Peace Therapy

This book is part of the Abbey Press
line of products that proclaim

Peace begins here™

It has been crafted with care
and with the conviction that:

- The human family yearns for peace.
- For peace to exist between groups of people,
it must first exist within the individual heart.
- Inner peace is essential
for human happiness, fulfillment, and growth.
- God cares, saves, and is near,
and we are called to be
God's peace-giving
presence to each other.

35.

To be a woman is to be
life-giving, life-sustaining,
life-protecting, life-changing,
life-rejoicing. Celebrate
your womanhood!

Be-good-to-your-body Therapy
#20188-9 $3.95   ISBN 0-87029-255-2

Celebrate-your-womanhood Therapy
  (new, improved binding)
#20189-7 $4.95   ISBN 0-87029-254-4

Acceptance Therapy (color edition)
#20182-2 $5.95   ISBN 0-87029-259-5

Acceptance Therapy (regular edition)
#20190-5 $3.95   ISBN 0-87029-245-5

Keeping-up-your-spirits Therapy
#20195-4 $3.95   ISBN 0-87029-242-0

Play Therapy
#20200-2 $3.95   ISBN 0-87029-233-1

Slow-down Therapy
#20203-6 $3.95   ISBN 0-87029-229-3

One-day-at-a-time Therapy
#20204-4 $3.95   ISBN 0-87029-228-5

Prayer Therapy (new, improved binding)
#20206-9 $4.95   ISBN 0-87029-225-0

Be-good-to-your-marriage Therapy
  (new, improved binding)
#20205-1 $4.95   ISBN 0-87029-224-2

Be-good-to-yourself Therapy (hardcover)
#20196-2 $10.95   ISBN 0-87029-243-9

Be-good-to-yourself Therapy
  (new, improved binding)
#20255-6 $4.95   ISBN 0-87029-209-9

Available at your favorite bookstore or directly from us
at One Caring Place, Abbey Press Publications,
St. Meinrad, IN 47577.
Phone orders: Call 1-800-325-2511

Karen Katafiasz is a writer and editor. She is the author of *Finding Your Way Through Grief, Celebrate-your-womanhood Therapy, Grief Therapy, Christmas Therapy*, and *Self-esteem Therapy*. A native of Toledo, Ohio, she now lives in Santa Claus, Indiana.

Illustrator for the Abbey Press Elf-help Books, **R.W. Alley** also illustrates and writes children's books. He lives in Barrington, Rhode Island, with his wife, daughter, and son.

The Story of the Abbey Press Elves

The engaging figures that populate the Abbey Press "elf-help" line of publications and products first appeared in 1987 on the pages of a small self-help book called *Be-good-to-yourself Therapy*. Shaped by the publishing staff's vision and defined in R.W. Alley's inventive illustrations, they lived out author Cherry Hartman's gentle, self-nurturing advice with charm, poignancy, and humor.

Reader response was so enthusiastic that more Elf-help Books were soon under way, a still-growing series that has inspired a line of related gift products.

The especially endearing character featured in the early books—sporting a cap with a mood-changing candle in its peak—has since been joined by a spirited female elf with flowers in her hair.

These two exuberant, sensitive, resourceful, kindhearted, lovable sprites, along with their lively elfin community, reveal what's truly important as they offer messages of joy and wonder, playfulness and co-creation, wholeness and serenity, the miracle of life and the mystery of God's love.

With wisdom and whimsy, these little creatures with long noses demonstrate the elf-help way to a rich and fulfilling life.

Elf-help Books…adding "a little character" and a lot of help to self-help reading!

Anger Therapy (new, improved binding)
#20127-7 $4.95   ISBN 0-87029-292-7

Caregiver Therapy (new, improved binding)
#20164-0 $4.95   ISBN 0-87029-285-4

Self-esteem Therapy (new, improved binding)
#20165-7 $4.95   ISBN 0-87029-280-3

Take-charge-of-your-life Therapy
  (new, improved binding)
#20168-1 $4.95   ISBN 0-87029-271-4

Work Therapy (new, improved binding)
#20166-5 $4.95   ISBN 0-87029-276-5

Everyday-courage Therapy
#20167-3 $3.95   ISBN 0-87029-274-9

Peace Therapy
#20176-4 $3.95   ISBN 0-87029-273-0

Friendship Therapy
#20174-9 $3.95   ISBN 0-87029-270-6

Christmas Therapy (color edition)
#20175-6 $5.95   ISBN 0-87029-268-4

Grief Therapy
#20178-0 $3.95   ISBN 0-87029-267-6

More Be-good-to-yourself Therapy
#20180-6 $3.95   ISBN 0-87029-262-5

Happy Birthday Therapy
#20181-4 $3.95   ISBN 0-87029-260-9

Forgiveness Therapy (new, improved binding)
#20184-8 $4.95   ISBN 0-87029-258-7

Keep-life-simple Therapy
#20185-5 $3.95   ISBN 0-87029-257-9

Peace Therapy

written by
Carol Ann Morrow

illustrated by
R.W. Alley

ONE
CARING
PLACE
Abbey Press

Text © 1995 Carol Ann Morrow
Illustrations © 1995 St. Meinrad Archabbey
Published by One Caring Place
Abbey Press
St. Meinrad, Indiana 47577

Library of Congress Catalog Number
94-96664

ISBN 0-87029-273-0

Printed in the United States of America

Foreword

"Lord, make me an instrument of your peace." So begins the well-known prayer of St. Francis of Assisi.

For a time, Francis lived the life of a knight, which, for all its chivalry and romantic ideals, also included battles and prisons. It was in prison that Francis embraced a new mission, a mission that we might today call "Peace Therapy."

He turned from an outer knighthood that protected the peace of Assisi to an inner commitment to become a person of peace. As he grew in peace, he was able to tame a wolf, challenge a sultan, and greet the violence of Sister Death with a word of welcome.

Reflecting on our own place in God's peace, we can see how every global conflict begins with fear, envy, anger, mistrust, and deceit.

How can we decry violence on our streets and war in foreign lands when our hearts harbor the same feelings of aggression? We can expect the outer world to mirror our inner turmoil—and it does.

Peace Therapy is a pocket-size declaration of peace in words and pictures. May it help you to achieve peace within and to live out peace with your entire being—body, mind, heart, soul.

1.

Be at peace with yourself. Even as God calls you to growth and progress, God loves you as you are. You have worth beyond measure, for you are a child of God.

2.

Don't make war with parts of yourself that you can't change. Accept your shadow side, your brokenness, your weaknesses, as well as your strengths. Inner peace unifies the parts into wholeness.

3.

Ground yourself in values that you've chosen with intent and deliberation. Then determine where your own attitudes and actions are at war with those values. Only you can end the conflict.

4.

Recognize if you've made
resentment, distrust, hostility
your armor against a world that
has hurt you in the past.
Commit yourself to remove this
armor, piece by piece.

5.

Unclench your jaw and your fists and drop your weapons. When your posture is tense, guarded, and wary, you are preparing for battle, not for peace. Let your body be a diplomatic envoy in a world seeking peace.

6.

Maintaining an enemies list taxes your energy and hardens your heart. Look for the good that God sees; love your enemies. When there are no enemies left, there will be peace.

7.

Disturbing the peace is a crime. When you rant and rave and stomp and fret over life's petty grievances, arrest yourself!

8.

When there's someone with whom you have conflicts, begin to make peace in your imagination. Picture yourself at peace. Slowly enlarge the image to include the other person. Put that picture in your mind's pocket and look at it with love now and then.

9.

Work through your anger. Those who hurt you do so out of their own insecurity, ignorance, and weakness, not strength. Be strong and move beyond your anger toward forgiveness.

10.

Accept responsibility for the times when you've hurt others because you lacked inner peace. Make amends to them when you can.

11.

Kicking the cat, slamming the door, honking your horn in complaint are not the postures of peace. Be aware of how your unexamined feelings burst forth in inappropriate ways. Deal with those feelings.

12.

Peace sees similarities among people, not threatening differences that form barriers. Identify a difference—a value, an attitude, a choice—that threatens you. Don't judge that difference, but seek to understand it.

13.

Terrible wars have begun over the control of territory and the exercise of power. Consider your own need to possess and have power over others. The more you can let go of this need, the less reason you have to disturb the peace by acts of violence. You can become a bridge instead of a border patrol.

14.

Speak gently. If you hear violence in your language, it comes from a place within your heart. Choose the vocabulary of peace and serenity over words of damnation, curses, woe, and complaint.

15.

Use a gentle voice to call family
members to the telephone, for
dinner, or from play. Invite
rather than command;
anticipate cooperation rather
than resistance. Be patient.
Peace comes on soft wings, not
in a thundering stampede.

16.

Measure your words of judgment. People seldom benefit from harsh criticism of their character or actions. Choose words of praise and acceptance, words that build peace.

17.

Be at peace with your circumstances. Allow what you have no power over to just be as it is. Where you do have power and something needs changing, do what you can and then let go. You don't have to fix everything.

18.

Declare a personal buffer zone. Make one corner of your home a haven, a sanctuary. When you feel your temper fraying and hear your voice rising, take time out there—perhaps with a book, a poster, or an object that whispers peace to your heart.

19.

Treasure the peace of your past. Remember the times and places you have known peace, and return there in reality or in your heart. Bring the feeling, the grace of those moments to today's challenges.

20.

Let your heart be untroubled. Even though you can't see the end of a difficult time, soothe your heart with confidence in a Power beyond yourself.

21.

Peace can be disturbed by too much coming and going. Decide which people and projects you want to invite into your day. Give other "visitors" appointments for tomorrow, next week, or next year. Then enjoy what you've chosen to give your attention to.

22.

Passive acceptance of injustice is not peace; it is a threat to peace. Recognize the threat and work for justice. But take care to avoid methods that are as unpeaceful and unjust as what you're trying to eliminate.

23.

Being at peace is not the same as being placid. You can be assertive, firm, even passionate and bold, yet be at peace. Peace is deeper than the quiet of inaction. Peace requires your participation.

24.

Listening to others express their feelings—including anger—is an act of peace. Don't hear just to determine when you can inject your own words. When you're fully present in your listening, you invite another to locate the peace within.

25.

Peace is not simply a bouquet you can hand to a friend. You can, however, be that bouquet yourself. And the fragrance may entice others to transplant tiny seedlings of peace in their own hearts.

26.

You don't have to "make" peace yourself, but simply allow the peace of God—already present—to flow through you to others. If you block its gentle current, you force it to chart a course around you. Be a channel of peace.

27.

Call a day's truce if peace seems too much to achieve. For twenty-four hours, hold your fire, lower your weapons, let down your guard, and relax. Practice peace one day at a time.

28.

Your peacekeeping may be local, but it's the same as an international mission: to stop sniping, lay down arms, talk face-to-face, agree on basic principles, honor the agreement. With practice, you can declare your life a demilitarized zone.

29.

Practice random acts of kindness. They will strengthen the fainthearted, confuse the hardhearted, and comfort the disheartened.

30.

Choose your own peace theme—a favorite song or hymn or poem or prayer. Hum, sing, read, or say it when you feel under siege.

31.

Just as Native Americans share the pipe of peace, you can create a moment of peace by sharing something of your own: a flower, a cookie, a handwritten note, a greeting card. Your act builds a positive and peaceful atmosphere.

32.

Search for signs of peace:
conflicts resolved, families
reunited, people helping people,
people joining arms instead of
bearing them. The angels'
chorus of "Peace on Earth"
still resounds. Let its melody
sustain your hope.

33.

Every day, imagine the world at peace. Imagine open borders, free and fair trade, weapons melted into plows and hoes. Every invention, every action, was first imagined. Think peace.

34.

Peace is as real as the clouds,
which—though they appear
wispy and insubstantial—hold
power and blessings for the
earth. As they grace the sky, so
will peace grace the earth.
Believe in the possibility, the
reality of peace.

35.

To make peace, you must be at peace. Peace begins in each individual heart. Blessed are the peacemakers.

Carol Ann Morrow is the author of two *CareNotes*, also published by Abbey Press, and the editor of *Youth Update*, a publication for teenagers. Married, she is an associate member of the Sisters of St. Francis, Oldenburg, Indiana. Through her peaceful husband and through the Franciscan friars and sisters, she has learned much about peace.

Illustrator for the Abbey Press Elf-help Books, **R.W. Alley** also illustrates and writes children's books. He lives in Barrington, Rhode Island, with his wife, daughter, and son.

The Story of the Abbey Press Elves

The engaging figures that populate the Abbey Press "elf-help" line of publications and products first appeared in 1987 on the pages of a small self-help book called *Be-good-to-yourself Therapy*. Shaped by the publishing staff's vision and defined in R.W. Alley's inventive illustrations, they lived out author Cherry Hartman's gentle, self-nurturing advice with charm, poignancy, and humor.

Reader response was so enthusiastic that more Elf-help Books were soon under way, a still-growing series that has inspired a line of related gift products.

The especially endearing character featured in the early books—sporting a cap with a mood-changing candle in its peak—has since been joined by a spirited female elf with flowers in her hair.

These two exuberant, sensitive, resourceful, kindhearted, lovable sprites, along with their lively elfin community, reveal what's truly important as they offer messages of joy and wonder, playfulness and co-creation, wholeness and serenity, the miracle of life and the mystery of God's love.

With wisdom and whimsy, these little creatures with long noses demonstrate the elf-help way to a rich and fulfilling life.

Elf-help Books

...adding "a little character" and a lot of help to self-help reading!

Teacher Therapy
#20145 $4.95   ISBN 0-87029-302-8

Live-from-your-soul Therapy
#20146 $4.95   ISBN 0-87029-303-6

Be-good-to-your-family Therapy
#20154 $4.95   ISBN 0-87029-300-1

Stress Therapy
#20153 $4.95   ISBN 0-87029-301-X

Making-sense-out-of-suffering Therapy
#20156 $4.95   ISBN 0-87029-296-X

Get Well Therapy
#20157 $4.95   ISBN 0-87029-297-8

Anger Therapy
#20127 $4.95   ISBN 0-87029-292-7

Caregiver Therapy
#20164 $4.95   ISBN 0-87029-285-4

Self-esteem Therapy
#20165 $4.95   ISBN 0-87029-280-3

Take-charge-of-your-life Therapy
#20168 $4.95   ISBN 0-87029-271-4

Work Therapy
#20166 $4.95   ISBN 0-87029-276-5

Everyday-courage Therapy
#20167 $4.95   ISBN 0-87029-274-9

Peace Therapy
#20176 $4.95   ISBN 0-87029-273-0

Friendship Therapy
#20174 $4.95   ISBN 0-87029-270-6

Christmas Therapy (color edition)
#20175 $5.95   ISBN 0-87029-268-4

Grief Therapy
#20178 $4.95   ISBN 0-87029-267-6

More Be-good-to-yourself Therapy
#20180 $3.95   ISBN 0-87029-262-5

Happy Birthday Therapy
#20181 $4.95   ISBN 0-87029-260-9

Forgiveness Therapy
#20184 $4.95   ISBN 0-87029-258-7

Keep-life-simple Therapy
#20185 $4.95   ISBN 0-87029-257-9

Be-good-to-your-body Therapy
#20188 $4.95   ISBN 0-87029-255-2

Celebrate-your-womanhood Therapy
#20189 $4.95   ISBN 0-87029-254-4

Acceptance Therapy (color edition)
#20182 $5.95   ISBN 0-87029-259-5

Acceptance Therapy
#20190 $4.95   ISBN 0-87029-245-5

Keeping-up-your-spirits Therapy
#20195 $4.95   ISBN 0-87029-242-0

Play Therapy
#20200 $4.95   ISBN 0-87029-233-1

Slow-down Therapy
#20203 $4.95   ISBN 0-87029-229-3

One-day-at-a-time Therapy
#20204 $4.95   ISBN 0-87029-228-5

Prayer Therapy
#20206 $4.95   ISBN 0-87029-225-0

Be-good-to-your-marriage Therapy
#20205 $4.95   ISBN 0-87029-224-2

Be-good-to-yourself Therapy (hardcover)
#20196 $10.95   ISBN 0-87029-243-9

Be-good-to-yourself Therapy
#20255 $4.95   ISBN 0-87029-209-9

Available at your favorite bookstore or directly
from us at: One Caring Place, Abbey Press
Publications, St. Meinrad, IN 47577.
Or call 1-800-325-2511.